KID SCIENTIST
Archaeologists on a Dig

Sue Fliess

illustrated by Mia Powell

Albert Whitman & Company
Chicago, Illinois

To all the budding archaeologists;
keep digging for the truth—SF

To Tom and my wonderful family
for always encouraging me to
keep chasing my dreams—MP

Library of Congress Cataloging-in-Publication data
is on file with the publisher.

Text copyright © 2022 by Sue Fliess
Illustrations copyright © 2022 by Albert Whitman & Company
Illustrations by Mia Powell
First published in the United States of America
in 2022 by Albert Whitman & Company
ISBN 978-0-8075-4157-9 (hardcover)
ISBN 978-0-8075-4155-5 (ebook)

Printed in China
10 9 8 7 6 5 4 3 2 1 WKT 26 25 24 23 22 21

For more information about Albert Whitman & Company,
visit our website at www.albertwhitman.com.

"Who wants to travel back in time?" Sam asks his team of archaeologists as they all prepare for their first day of digging in Cambodia.

"After months of research, we're finally at the world's biggest religious temple: Angkor Wat!" Mika exclaims.

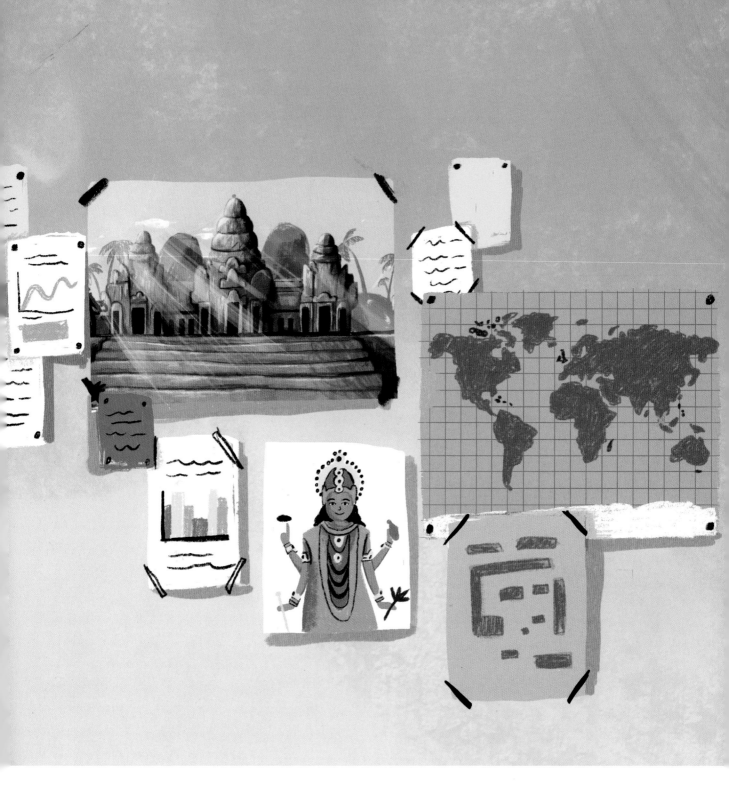

Sam's team is hoping to find artifacts, which are objects left behind by ancient people. Archaeologists study artifacts to learn more about history and people who lived a long time ago.

When the team arrives at the temple, they stop to admire it.

"I knew the temple was large, but now that we're here, it looks massive!" says Tara.

"The Khmer people built this temple around the twelfth century and dedicated it to the Hindu god Vishnu," says Johan. He reads off some other background information they learned before their trip. "At the temple, we know that they made and used pottery, carved drawings, and built statues."

Even though it's called a dig, archaeologists actually remove dirt slowly and carefully, layer by layer, so they don't damage any artifacts they uncover and so they can document the whole process.

"Pass me the string," calls Tara as she and Johan start to create a measured grid over their work area. The grid helps the team keep track of exactly which square they find objects in.

Johan takes pictures of the whole site, creating a photo log to study later.

Mika starts taking notes about everything they discover. "Find anything yet?" she asks.

"Do animal droppings count?" asks Tara, who is sifting through the dirt with a sieve, a screen-like tool that separates smaller particles from larger ones. "Because that's all I've found, so far."

Using the sieve lets her catch even the tiniest artifact fragments, like beads or other small remains.

As Sam sweeps deeper with a small brush, something catches the light. "Come quick," he says. "I found something!" The team rushes over to see.

"Maybe it's art," says Johan, "like a statue."
"Or pottery," says Tara.
"Whatever it is," says Sam, "it could be important."

Together, the team carefully brushes, scrapes, and sifts away more dirt while also taking photos and notes. Soon they've uncovered several pieces of decorated pottery buried three feet below the surface.

"You were both right," says Sam. "It's art *and* pottery. And it looks like these pieces may all be part of one large pot."

The four archaeologists then gently free the pieces from the ground.

Once the pieces are labeled with their grid locations and photographed, the team carries them to the tent for analysis.

Tara remarks that the pot is made of clay, so when it was first made, it was heated to high temperatures, or fired. This process makes the clay hard and strong.

Mika notes that some of the pieces are decorated with parts of a face. "Could this be an image of Vishnu?"

Johan pulls out his book about Angkor Wat. "Look here," he says, showing the team. "This piece looks like part of Vishnu's crown, and these pieces show some of his face."

VISHNU

"Archaeology is like putting together pieces of a giant puzzle," says Sam.

"In this case, the puzzle is a pot," says Tara.

"And the pot is a clue to the past," adds Mika.

Sam places the labeled pieces in sealed plastic bags, and everyone heads to the nearby lab. On the way, they start to develop a hypothesis, or a guess based on evidence, about the pot's age.

"Could we use the spot dating method to estimate how old the pot is?" asks Mika.

"Great idea," says Sam. "Since we already know that the Khmer people lived at Angkor Wat between the twelfth and fifteenth centuries, we can guess the pot's age based on that history."

"That means the pot could be about nine hundred years old," says Johan.

"That's a good guess," says Tara. "But how will we know if it's right?"

"We'll have to get cooking!" says Sam.

"Great," says Johan. "I'm hungry!"

"Not *that* kind of cooking," says Tara. "We're going to crush a test piece and reheat it to find a more exact age of the pot."

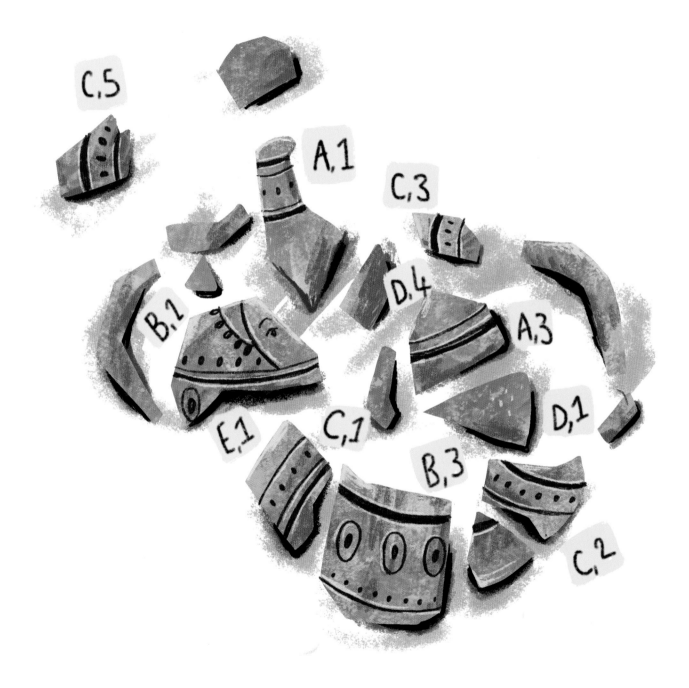

"It's a technique called thermoluminescence dating, or TL," says Sam. "*Thermo* meaning heat; *luminescence* meaning light. We can use it to figure out the ages of objects that were heated a long time ago, like pottery, lava, or even dirt and rocks that were once warmed by sunlight."

"So it will tell us when our pot was originally fired by humans?" asks Mika.

"Exactly," says Sam. "When the pot is reheated now, it will release light. The TL machine measures the exact amount of light that is released, and from those numbers, we can calculate how long it's been since our pot last got really hot—in this case, when it was made."

Sam heats the broken sample in the TL machine.
The team watches and waits.
"The pieces are glowing!" says Mika.

When the process is complete, the team reviews the machine's measurements.

"Based on these measurements," says Sam, "the pot we found is eight hundred and seventy years old!"

"That supports our hypothesis," says Tara.

"I wonder what the pot was used for," says Johan.

"Well, the Khmer people's agriculture was mainly rice and fish," says Mika, "so maybe this pot was used to store food."

The team organizes their new data, shares it with other archaeologists at the dig site, then plans to excavate the rest of their grid over the next week. When they finish digging, they will write up and publish their research so other scientists and historians can learn more about Angkor Wat's history.

"Rice and fish sounds delicious," says Johan. "*Now* can we eat?"
The team breaks for a well-deserved meal.

"Dig in!"

WHAT IS AN ARCHAEOLOGIST?

An archaeologist's job is to learn about people of the past by digging up and examining ancient things that the people left behind. Archaeologists hope that each piece will give them clues as to what life was like and how people lived during a particular time.

There are two main branches of archaeology: historical archaeology, which studies civilizations that left behind written records, and prehistoric archaeology, which studies societies that did not have writing systems.

All scientists research by following the steps of the scientific method. Sam and his team used each step to guide their research.

STEPS OF THE SCIENTIFIC METHOD

1. Make an observation and do background research. Before Sam and his team went to Angkor Wat in Cambodia, they did research on the ancient civilizations that once inhabited the temple city.

2. Ask questions about the observations and gather information. After observing a piece of pottery, Sam asked how old it was.

3. Form a hypothesis. Sam first hypothesized that the pot was approximately nine hundred years old, but he wanted a more exact age of the pot.

4. Perform an experiment and collect data. Sam and his team used spot dating and thermoluminescence to pinpoint the pot's age.

5. Analyze the data and draw conclusions. Consider how the conclusions support or disprove the hypothesis. The team's analysis showed that the pottery was eight hundred and seventy years old and could have been used to hold rice. This supported his hypothesis.

6. Communicate or present your findings. After gathering more data, Sam and his team shared their data with others at the site and will publish their research so others can learn more about Angkor Wat's fascinating history.

HOW CAN I BECOME AN ARCHAEOLOGIST?

Do you love finding buried treasure? Maybe you'll be an archaeologist! Archaeologists come from many backgrounds and study geology, biology, or even art.

There are many ways to learn about archaeology, even before you study it in school:

- Check out books at your local library or watch historical documentaries.

- Visit a natural history museum or a museum with artifacts on display.

- Find out if there is a dig happening near you—you may be surprised to find that there is. They might need volunteers!

- Have a metal detector? Try it in your yard, the beach, or a park to see what buried treasure you can find. Always get permission first.

- Find a cut tree trunk and count the rings. The number of rings shows how old the tree is. The space between the rings shows its yearly growth.

If you want to become an archaeologist when you grow up, be sure to work hard in math, science, English, and history. Archaeologists need excellent research and writing skills, and use mathematical and statistical concepts in the field and for data analysis. You'll need to be a good communicator, too, to share results with fellow archaeologists and the public. After you graduate high school, you'll need a bachelor of science (BS) or a bachelor of arts (BA) degree from college. Choose a college that offers majors in archaeology or anthropology. You'll get classroom instruction, train in the archaeological field, and learn laboratory techniques. Maybe you'll even get to go on a dig, like Sam does!

SUGGESTED READING FOR KIDS

Farndon, John. *100 Things You Should Know about Archeology*. Broomall, PA: Mason Crest, 2011.

Panchyk, Richard. *Archaeology for Kids: Uncovering the Mysteries of Our Past: 25 Activities*. Chicago: Chicago Review, 2001.

Steele, Kathryn. *Stones and Bones: Archaeology in Action*. New York: PowerKids, 2013.